ACES
PAST

ACES PAST

Christopher Shores
and Patrick Bunce

MILITARY PRESS
New York

A Salamander Book

©Salamander Books Ltd 1991

This 1991 edition published by Military
Press and distributed by Outlet Book
Company, Inc., a Random House
Company, 225 Park Avenue South,
New York, New York 10003.

Printed and bound in Italy

ISBN 0-517-03589-8

87654321

Photo Credits
The publishers would like to thank
the following individuals and
organizations for their assistance in
producing this book: The Battle of
Britain Memorial Flight; Derek Bunce;
The Champlin Fighter Musuem, Mesa,
Arizona; Paul Coggan; The Collings
Foundation; The Combat Jets
Museum, Houston, Texas; Rod Dean;
Jeff Ethell; Spencer Flack, Myrick
Aviation Services; Arthur Gibson and
Paul Warren Wilson, Plain Sailing;
Stephen Grey, The Fighter Collection;
Mark and Ray Hanna, The Old Flying
Machine Company; Norman Lees; Bob
Mitchell; John Pitchforth, Nikon U.K.;
Lee Proudfoot; David Putnam, Eric
Rattray and Susan D'Arcy, Enigma
Films Ltd; John Romain, The Aircraft
Restoration Company; Royal Air Force
Command, Public Relations; The
Shuttleworth Collection, Old Warden
Aerodrome, Bedfordshire; Coke
Stewart; Graham Warner, The British
Aerial Musuem; Herschel Whittington
and Russ Anderson, The Confederate
Air Force, Harlingen, Texas; and Keith
Wilson.

All the colour photographs were taken
by Patrick Bunce using Nikon cameras
and lenses supplied by Nikon U.K. and
Kodachrome film from Kodak U.K.

Black-and-white material is from the
Salamander Archives if not credited to
the following copyright sources: Alex
Imrie Collection, page 12, 17, 18;
Imperial War Museum, 29, 58, 61, 63,
76, 128, 137; Pilot Press, 83, 138; RAF
Musuem, 77, 92; Smithsonian
Institution, 30, 38, 44, 46, 65, 67, 70, 80,
94, 106, 107, 110, 140/141; US National
Archives, 32, 49, 55, 90, 94, 112, 116,
118, 123, 127, 131, 143, 155, 157.

Endpapers: B-17 ''Memphis Belle''
Page 1: Spanish-built Messerschimitt
109 and Spitfire
2/3: A '109' hotly pursued by a Spitfire
and a Hurricane
4/5: P-51s, P-40 and P-47 in the
Harlingen flypast

6: Se5 and DrI in mock dogfight
7: (top) Bristol Fighter;
(bottom) Russian Polikarpov Po2 with
French roundel
8: Buchon HA 1112
9: (top) Spitfires; (bottom) B-17s
10/11: (top) B-25; (bottom) Spitfires

Introduction

THE FIFTIETH anniversary of the outbreak of World War Two has now passed, but a lengthy series of commemorations will continue until mid-1995 as people around the world remember significant events in the recent history of their countries. And what has proved to be the highlight of these affairs? Arguably, it has been the spirited air displays provided by the surviving aircraft of the time, the distinct rumbling note of their engines evoking an era of combat so different from that of their more powerful, ear-splitting jet-engined successors.

Summer 1990 and the Battle of Britain anniversary displays have seen countless instances of yesteryear's elderly warbirds passing overhead in nostalgic array. These occasions never cease to enthrall the modern spectator and both in Europe and the United States there has grown a highly appreciative audience for propeller and jet-engine 'aces of the past'. The Con-

federate Air Force in Texas has an enthusiastic membership which has managed to equip itself with so many planes that it now has a larger inventory than many of the world's national air forces. The film "Memphis Belle" has drawn large crowds to the cinema who have admired the bravery of 1940's youth as they made their way to death and destruction over western Europe in the stately Boeing B-17 Flying Fortress.

Is it just nostalgia for a mythical past deemed to be simpler, more straightforward than our complex, technological present will allow with its instant, worldwide media coverage? Or is it something more than this?

Aircraft were considered too new in the inter-war period for them to be consigned to museums; they were too redolent of progess. Conversely, after World War Two the world was too weary of warfare to be reminded of the recent past. It was

only in the 1960s, after a decade or so of relative peace, that the 'trend' really began, perhaps sparked by the sudden and almost complete transition from the whirling propeller of the piston-engine to the rowdiness of the jet.

Initially, just a few wartime aircraft made appearances at air shows, having been discovered and made airworthy. Their impact on the audiences was such that their numbers began to grow as more and more were searched out and restored. Primarily these were fighters acquired for the aerial racing circuit in the United States — Chance Vought Corsairs, Grumman Bearcats, Hawker Sea Furies and North American Mustangs. It soon broadened, however, with museums showing increasing interest and an enormous growth in the availability of, and market for, plastic model kits.

Placed in static museum displays, most of these genuine, unmodified wartime

aircraft were painted in spurious colours and markings which revealed that little more than nominal research had taken place. The airworthy examples often flew emblazoned with civil registrations and lacking the wartime accoutrements that would have made them so authentic. Help was at hand, however, in the shape of organizations such as the Shuttleworth Trust based at Old Warden airfield in Bedfordshire, England. They were beginning to show really old aircraft — of World War One vintage or older — and they flew them after having restored them very carefully, taking great pains to match every detail of their former glory. Such dedicated work touched a nerve with the viewing public.

Further impetus was given by a series of big films which needed relevant aircraft and expert advisers to ensure that the productions — "Battle of Britain", "Tora, Tora, Tora", "Midway" and "The Blue Max" — achieved high standards of technical and visual accuracy. The audiences worldwide, growing in their sophistication, would be satisfied with nothing less. Thus it was that German aircraft were found still flying with the Spanish Air Force and were purchased in large numbers, British and American fighters were made airworthy, and Japanese replicas were built around

similar extant models. The boom now began in earnest!

Until then it had seemed that supplies of the relevant aircraft types were limited, especially those which were of sufficiently high quality to offer more than a static display in a museum. Yet very soon enthusiasts had discovered even bigger types: in the United States a number of elderly 'water bombers', used by rural fire services to quell forest fires proved to be B-17s, and in the Far East much-modified Avro Lancaster bombers and Short Sunderland flying-boats were discovered. Restoration of the big, four-engined 'birds' had become a reality.

The modern, more knowledgeable 'fan' demanded that the aircraft be painted accurately, that extraneous modifications be removed and that guns, sights and armoured windscreens all be fitted. A new breed was taking over and now the search was really on in barns and remote, forgotten airstrips, scrapyards, farms etc.

These efforts resulted in a huge variety of old aircraft being discovered. Japanese fighters and bombers were sought in the steaming, fetid jungles of New Guinea and the South Pacific islands. If complete aircraft could not be found, in stepped the aviation archaeologists, a new group who tracked down wartime crash sites over a period of months or sometimes years of

patient and painstaking research. Once a site had been located they carefully excavated, hoping to recover as much as possible of the crashed aircraft. Water has proved no barrier to these intrepid volunteers and the depths of Norwegian fjords and Scottish lochs have been scoured by sub-aqua teams. From such watery graves have emerged some of the more esoteric types such as a Gloster Gladiator biplane, a Blackburn Skua, a Handley Page Halifax and more recently a Vickers Wellington.

The energy, innovation, enthusiasm and commitment of these restoration teams the world over is admirable, and their dedication is unsurpassed. Countless thousands of hours of work have gone into these painstaking rebuilds that have rendered airworthy many aircraft which even the greatest optimists had never dreamt they would see airborne again.

Such success has also raised questions about the future, and arguments have persisted to the present. Should these rare — often irreplaceable — examples be put at risk by flying them, or would it be wiser to maintain them as static displays so they can be enjoyed for many years to come? Beautiful and lovingly restored aircraft have been crashed and destroyed in recent years after just a few flights, notably the Bristol Bulldog, Macchi 202, Dewoitine D-520 and Bell P-63 Kingcobra. Perhaps where only one example of a type exists it should be preserved and not put at risk, but whenever several have survived or been restored then there can be little doubt — as the illustrations in this book demonstrate — that one or more should be flown.

It is a very different matter seeing such an aircraft in the sky rather than looking at it silent and still on the ground. In its true element with all the accompanying vibrancy, noise, colour and movement it provides an unforgettable experience. To hear the roar of the Pratt & Whitney radial engine and see it pull the P-47 Thunderbolt up into a climb, a roll, wing-over and a dive back again is truly to savour the aircraft as it should be seen and heard!

World War Two aircraft do not monopolize the air shows, there are many beautiful wood and canvas originals or replicas around of World War One vintage. Many continue to be built whenever suitable engines can be found to power them and provided the carpentry and needlework skills have not disappeared totally. There are also the survivors from the first generation of jets. Piloted in the 1950s by veterans of the recent world war, these more modern-looking aircraft were very active in Korea and some remained in service until the later war in Vietnam. Increasingly, they too became museum pieces and now the sleek F-86 Sabres, F9F

Panthers and MiG-15s have joined the display circuit and become crowd favourites.

The process is ongoing, the mighty F-4 Phantom and MiG-21 may remain in service with many of the world's air forces but they are now being sought by museums and will increasingly become historical items which will thrill crowds with re-enactments of their clashes in the skies over Vietnam.

Preserved or replicated, all the old warbirds are incredibly evocative; the bomber represents the memory of terrible sacrifice, while the fighter embodies one of the few opportunities that existed for individualism and chivalry in recent warfare. Today, in their growing millions, the public view a range of airworthy "aces" that are both exciting to watch and beautiful to look at. These marvellous aircraft deserve to be seen for a long time yet to come.

Originally designed as a reconnaissance and artillery-spotting machine with a capacity to defend itself against opposing fighters, the Bristol F2A and F2B two-seaters soon became known as the "Bristol Fighter". It was as fast as the single-seat fighters of the day, very manoeuvrable, and with the added benefit of a gunner behind the pilot it proved to be a highly effective aircraft. Following the war it was used in the Middle East and India (below).

Only one airworthy example survives and it is owned by the Shuttleworth Trust based at Old Warden, Bedfordshire, England. The Bristol Fighter was equipping 18 squadrons by the war's end; the aircraft at centre right belongs to 22 Squadron based at Vert Galant, western France in April 1918.

The Royal Aircraft Factory's SE5a was one of the truly great combat aircraft of WWI. It was fast for its day, tough and had a good ceiling. Most that fly today are replicas, such as the line-up at the Biggin Hill Airshow (left) or this French example, owned by the Jean Sallis Collection, seen at La Ferte Alois (right). The Shuttleworth Collection, however, maintains a beautiful original, seen here (top) during the sunset at Shuttleworth's evening display.

A dog-fight re-enactment during a display. A pair of SE5s latch quickly onto the tail of the more agile Fokker Triplane (above, left) and then they "shoot him down" (top) trailing smoke. The SE5 was armed with a nose-mounted Vickers and a Lewis gun above the wing. It was flown by many of the great "aces", men such as Mannock, McCudden, Beauchamp-Proctor, Bishop and Ball, as was the Sopwith Camel (above). The DrI and the Camel both belong to the Old Flying Machine Company.

The Fokker DrI Triplane — mount of the deadly "Red Baron" — was one of the most nimble fighters to see service during WWI. No originals survive, but a number of replicas have been built which delight crowds at airshows every year, such as

Bridging the gap between two eras, the Gloster Gladiator, the RAF's last fighter biplane, was a mixture of the old and the new. It had flying wires and a fixed undercarriage but an enclosed cockpit under a

these two flying at the annual
fighter meet held at North
Weald, England. Only a few
hundred were ever built, and
because they were in
demand from the German
"aces," air-worthiness was
vital, especially during the
winter (bottom left).

(Overleaf) A Fokker DrI
owned by the Old Flying
Machine Company, based
at Duxford, Cambridgeshire,
and painted in the markings
of von Richthofen's Circus-
Jagdgeschwader I.

The Curtiss P-40 Warhawk (known to the British as the Tomahawk) was available to the US in the greatest numbers when war broke out in 1941. It was a durable aircraft with good firepower and had seen action with the American Volunteer Group ("The Flying Tigers") aiding Chiang Kai-Shek's Chinese Nationalist forces in Burma. Later reinforcements were provided by the P-40 E Kittyhawk model. The National Warplane Museum has a flying P-40 (top left, bottom right and overleaf) which has been painted to represent just such an aircraft. At centre is a P-40E from a USAAF training unit winging over to begin an attack dive.

The nose design of the P-40 made it a particularly suitable fighter for the painting of shark's and dragon's teeth to add an air of menace (above and previous page). The "Rose Marie" (left) is one of a line of P-40s from 23rd Fighter Group of 14th Air Force all similarly painted in this way during late 1942.

The Chinese Nationalist insignia on the wings are clearly visible in this picture (left) taken at the Manchester Airshow, New Hampshire, USA.

The RAF's Desert Air Force also flew the P-40 (right, top and bottom), as did Australia, China, New Zealand and the USSR.

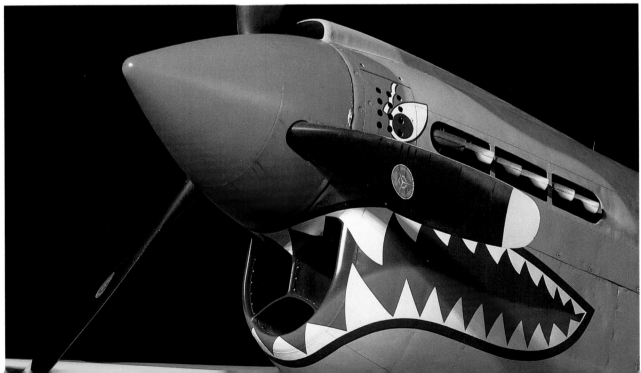

North American's P-51 Mustang was one of the greatest fighters of WWII and a superlative escort aircraft. Nearly 15,000 were built, and in Europe alone it flew more than 200,000 sorties, accounting for 5,000 Axis aircraft for losses of 2,500 P-51s. Most survivors are P-51Ds, such as that flown by Ray Hanna (left) of the Old Flying Machine Company with its white nose and bands typical of those used for recognition purposes. In formation or solo, P-51s can provide a colourful spectacle, such as these four at Duxford's Classic Fighter Display (bottom) and the close-up of the nose-art on Stephen Grey's ''Moose'' which evokes memories of a famed fighter from 357th Fighter Group.

A pair of beautifully restored P-51Ds (above and top), belonging to the Fighter Collection and the Old Flying Machine Company, in formation flight. In their wartime role (right) flying escort duty on distant B-17 and B-24 bombing raids disciplined flying was required to maintain protective defensive formations. Nose-art was a popular outlet for pilots and few come better than ''Glamorous Gen'' gleaming in the afternoon sun at Geneseo, New York.

AAF.SPEC.PROJ.NO.92778N
U.S. ARMY P-51D-5-NA
SERIAL NO. AAF 44-13903
CREW WEIGHT 200 LBS.

SERVICE THIS AIRPLANE WITH
GRADE 100/130 FUEL. IF NOT
AVAILABLE T.O. 05-5-1 WILL BE
CONSULTED FOR EMERGENCY ACTION

SUITABLE FOR AROMATIC FUEL

(Overleaf) Most Mustangs are flying in the USA but several are also to be found in the UK, among them Spencer Flack's red-nosed P-51D with bubble canopy.

At the time it entered service Republic's P-47 Thunderbolt was the largest, heaviest and most powerful single-engined fighter ever to fly. Steadily supplanted as a long-range escort by the P-51, the P-47 became the USAAF's premier fighter-bomber, causing chaos among Axis forces in Europe. Typical is this formation of bomb-laden P-47Ds over northern Italy late in the war (above). The Fighter Collection based at Duxford has restored a P-47D (previous page, top right and overleaf) and painted it to represent the 8th Air Force's 78th Fighter Group which was based there during the war (overleaf, top left).

Others exist too, among them a P-47N on the inventory of the Confederate Air Force based at Harlingen, Texas (previous page and far right).

A Bell P-63F Kingcobra belonging to the Confederate Air Force. Very few examples of this low-altitude fighter survive, but some are slowly being restored. Similar to the P-39 Aircobra, with an Allison engine located behind the pilot, most P-63s were supplied to the USSR under Lend-Lease. The Americans used it as a trainer, such as these in formation (left). It was well-armed with a heavy 37mm cannon in the nose and four .50in machine guns.

The Hurricane formed the backbone of RAF Fighter Command's strength in 1940 and they were far more active than the Spitfires. Stephen Grey's magnificent "Eagle" Squadron Hurricane (centre left and previous page) has been beautifully maintained and alongside his clipped wing Spitfire (right and centre right) it brings back memories of the fighter's heyday. Above and opposite are formations of Mark I Hurricanes in 1940.

The Spitfire served in most of the wartime campaigns. Several hundred were flown by the Americans in Italy until 1944; that of 31st Fighter Group (right) has crash landed at Salerno in 1943. Today, one of the most impressive groupings is the RAF's Battle of Britain Memorial Flight (top right), and it is common for British airshows to display a Spitfire-Hurricane combination. At Mildenhall (above) an Old Flying Machine Company Spitfire leads a Canadian Mark XVI with the "invasion band" markings of 1944 and a Hawker Hurricane of "Eagle" Squadron, the first American volunteer unit in the RAF.

Considered by many to be the most beautiful fighter aircraft ever to see service, the Supermarine Spitfire is certainly one of the most famous. In 1940 it was probably the only fighter in service which was truly a match for the Messerschmitt Bf 109E. They did much to keep the German fighters at bay, allowing the slower but more numerous Hurricanes to intercept the bombers. They captured the imagination of the British public and came to signify the spirit of defiance and the glamour of the young fighter ''ace''.

Quite a number of Spitfires are airworthy, both in the UK and the US, and up to 15 appeared at Battle of Britain Anniversary displays in England in 1990. This Spitfire IX, flown by Mark Hanna of the Old Flying Machine Company, has had its outer cannon stubs removed, giving it the appearance of an older Spitfire Mark V.

A German pilot's-eye-view of a pair of Spitfires (right) during a display at RAF Fighter Command's former premier fighter airfield at Biggin Hill, Kent. Below, a formation of Spitfire Is from 610 Squadron patrolling during the actual Battle of Britain. Far right is a lovely sunset at Binbrook, Lincolnshire which lights the bulky cowling of the Old Flying Machine Company's Spitfire IX.

The Fieseler Fi-156 Storch was a light STOL (Short Take Off and Landing) aircraft developed for liaison duties with the German Luftwaffe and Wehrmacht, a role it performed with distinction. It was produced in France after the war as the Morane-Saulnier MS-505 Criquet, an example of which is seen here painted to represent a headquarters Storch of Jagdgeschwader 54 ''Grunherz'' (Green Hearts), a Luftwaffe fighter unit.

With the greatest production figures ever for a fighter aircraft it is surprising that no original examples of the Messerschmitt Bf 109 are airworthy today. Currently, all that remain in flying condition are Spanish-built HA-1112 Buchons, although an accurate Bf 109 is being worked on. The difference lies in the nose and guns which were re-modelled to accomodate a non-Daimler engine and can be seen by comparing with the Bf 109E (top right) flying alongside the Ju87 Stuka over the Libyan desert during the war.

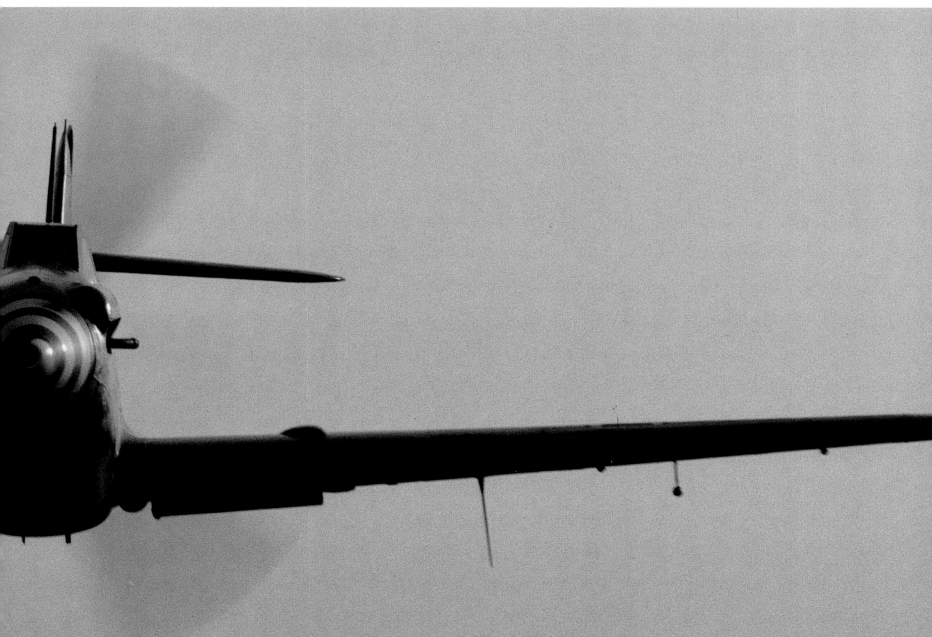

A pair of Bf 109 Fs (far right) show the position of the guns above the nose. The Buchon here has been accurately painted to resemble a Bf109G from a front-line unit in 1943. The yellow nose and white fuselage band are typical of the period, while the cross denotes a coveted Ritterkreuz has been awarded to the pilot.

Introduced in 1941, the Focke-Wulf Fw-190 had a distinct edge over the RAF's Spitfire Vs opposing it. By the time the US heavy bomber raids were underway in 1943 the Fw-190 fighter was the backbone of the Reich's defences. It was also developed as a fighter-bomber, the Fw-190G serving with units such as Schlachtageschwader 10 seen here over Romania in 1944 (top right). The Champlin Fighter Musuem, Mesa, Arizona has a restored Fw-190D9 on display. This "stretched" type began to appear in mid-1944 and carries the rear fuselage bands of the Home Defence.

Introduced to service over China in 1940, the Mitsubishi A6M Zero-Sen proved a complete and most unpleasant surprise to the Allies in 1941. It was without doubt the best carrier fighter in the world at that time, a position it held until 1943 and the arrival of Corsairs, Hellcats and P-38s which took advantage of its relative lack of armour protection. This rare example of a flying A6M-2 compares well with the 1942 original (top, left).

The Heinkel He-111 was one of the two most widely used bombers of WWII. A medium bomber, it played a major part in the notorious destruction of Guernica in Spain during the civil war and subsequently undertook similar operations over France and England in 1940. Ironically, it was in Spain that the He-111 survived longest, being produced there by Casa with Rolls-Royce Merlins. It is one of these that survives today rather than the Jumo-powered Luftwaffe version (top right).

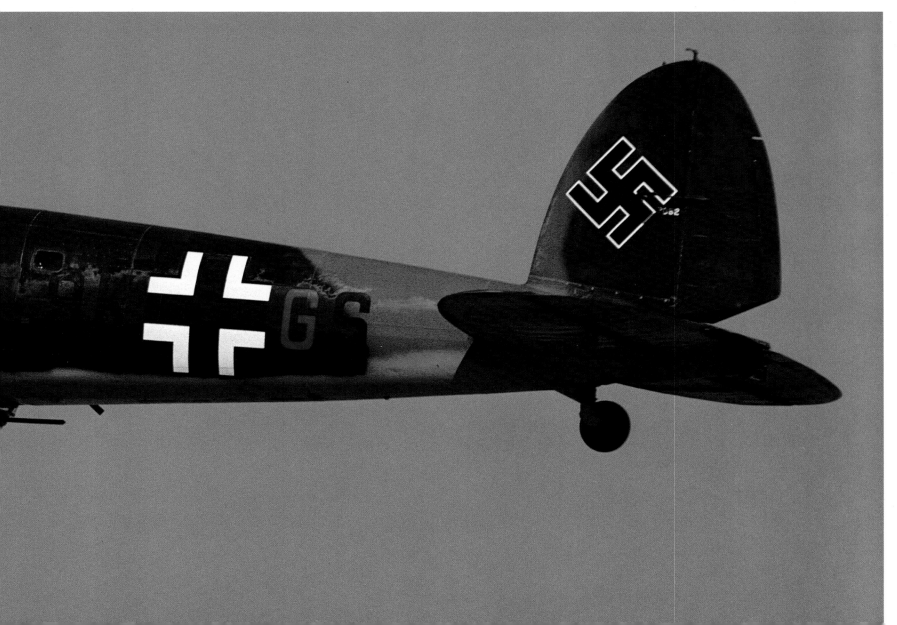

The RAF's best heavy bomber of WWII was the Avro Lancaster of "Dambusters" fame. Rugged and reliable, it could carry a massive load and its evolution culminated in the 22,000lb "Grand Slam" version. They made over 150,000 sorties, dropping more than 600,000 tons of bombs. Out of 7,000 built only two remain airworthy, one in Canada with the Canadian Warplane Heritage Collection (overleaf) and the other (below) with the RAF's Battle of Britain Memorial Flight.

The Lancaster undertook many long-range, high-altitude raids on Axis targets and was a principal component of the Allies' "Main Force" which, by 1944, was devastating Germany. Left: the bombing of a rocket site in northern France. Below, right: the famous "Dambusters" — 617 Squadron — with white painted upper surfaces prior to their transfer to the Far East as part of "Tiger Force".

The Boeing B-17 Flying Fortress is the best known US bomber of WWII. They were large, fast and high-flying but not well armed enough to merit their name. The B-17 contrail (bottom) became a familiar sight in the skies over East Anglia where many 8th Air Force bases were built during the war (right). Today, the story of the "Memphis Belle" has renewed interest in the B-17's exploits. A replica of the "Memphis Belle" is flying today (previous page); she was the first B-17 in 91st Bomb Group to complete 25 missions. Landing at dusk and flying high in the clouds, these preserved B-17s (far right, top and bottom) easily convey the atmosphere of those days while "Fuddy Duddy", belonging to the National Warplane Museum, offers a typically humorous example of nose-art.

Basking in the sunset the beauty of this B-17F can be appreciated (left). So too can the aircraft's power when viewed head-on at take-off (above).

When first acquired by the Army Air Corps in 1935 the Y1B-17 (right) had a slightly different tail and rudder design and fewer defensive turrets.

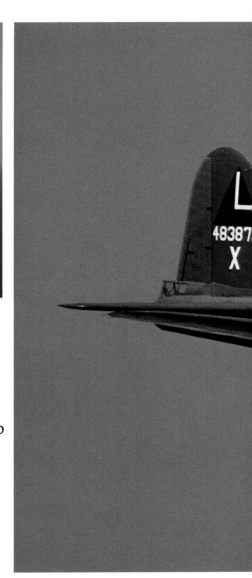

Dave Tallichet's "Memphis Belle" is not the only B-17 currently flying, the Confederate Air Force have a wonderful collection of all types of aircraft, including "Sentimental Journey" (overleaf) and "Texas Raiders" (right), a B-17G seen here with its P-51D escort. The paint schemes are from the 381st Bomb Group of 533rd Squadron and 55th Fighter Group of 343rd Squadron respectively. The profile (below) of the late Bob Richardson's B-17 provides a good view of its armament.

Over 18,000 Consolidated B-24 Liberators rolled off the lines during WWII, a mammoth figure and enough to equip 15 of the 8th Air Force's 41 bomber groups in Europe and to carry the burden of the war in the Far East from 1942 to 1944. These mighty aircraft could inflict great damage, as shown (top left) by this formation of B-24Ds over the refinery at Ploesti, Romania on 1 August 1943. Incredibly, only one airworthy B-24 has survived, lovingly restored by the Collings Foundation at a cost of $1.4 million. Seen head-on as it thunders into the air (previous page) this B-24H is an awesome aircraft. In profile (right) one can see on the fuselage the range of corporate sponsors who have made it all possible, indicating that projects of this nature are no longer the preserve of the dedicated amateur. The power-operated nose turret (top right) with its two 0.5in Brownings gives an idea of the defensive firepower available.

The tail-gunner's turret on "All American" has Brownings too (right), but the large bomber always remained vulnerable to enemy fire as the plumes of smoke (below) from a B-24J, downed when on a raid over Germany with the 8th Air Force in 1944, indicate. Even the interior has been restored to its wartime condition (right), as this rare photograph of the fuselage reveals (looking towards the rear). The yellow containers are oxygen for the crew. "Shoot You're Covered" (centre right) is a display B-24 at Pima Air Museum, Tucson, Arizona, another fine example of the prevalent nose-art.

The North American B-25 Mitchell was a twin-engined medium bomber flown by both the USAAF (far left and below, left) and the RAF (left and bottom, right). It was active in the Pacific, North Africa and Italy, with the RAF's 2nd Tactical Air Force using it widely in Europe.

The B-25 carried the name of the US Army Air Corps officer who had argued the pre-war case for the application of air power. Arguably the best of its class, it was the most produced American twin-engined aircraft of the war. Most served in the Pacific and were painted in colours similar to this typical US 5th Air Force scheme (far left, top and bottom). Many were also active in the Mediterranean and North African theatres, such as these B-25Js of 12th Air Force dropping a load of small bombs over northern Italy in 1944 (bottom right), or this preserved 9th Air Force example, "Yellow Rose", with desert markings (top right and overleaf).

The Martin B-26 Marauder first flew in November 1940 and saw initial service in the Pacific. Early heavy losses led to it being called the "Widow Maker", but modifications increased its popularity. This 9th Air Force colour scheme is a contrast to the natural metal finish with shark's mouth (bottom left).

"Carolyn" belongs to the
Confederate Air Force and is
currently the only one flying
in the world. Seen above
Texas, the Marauder's sleek
lines can be appreciated.

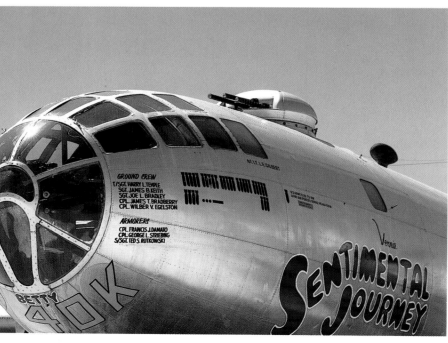

The Boeing B-29 Superfortress was introduced in June 1944 and it represented a tremendous leap forward in technology. With four powerful engines it had the speed of many fighters. "Fifi" (above and far left) is the only one remaining airworthy, although there are static displays such as "Betty/Sentimental Journey" at Pima (left).

In both flying-boat and amphibian form, the Consolidated PBY Catalina saw service in virtually every theatre of WWII. The "Cat" had an enormous endurance capability, being tasked to undertake long-range reconnaissance and anti-submarine patrols, most notably in the Pacific. Several remain airworthy today: the amphibian PBY (far right and top right) seen here is owned by the National Warplane Museum at Geneseo, New York, while the RAF Coastal Command version (right and overleaf), which lacks some authentic features, is owned by Plane Sailing based at Duxford. At top left is a late wartime "Cat" in US Naval Service.

The Douglas SBD Dauntless formed the backbone of the US Navy's carrier strike forces during the first two years of the Pacific War. It was active at the Coral Sea and Solomons battles, and at Midway it was instrumental in crippling the Japanese fleet. It was superseded by the SB2C Helldiver, but continued to serve until late in the war. This preserved SBD-3 (right) has been painted to represent US Navy Bombing Squadron VB-4 at the outbreak of the war; the late-model SBD-5s (top left) are flying over the US invasion fleet during the landings on Saipan, June 1944.

The Grumman F4F Wildcat was the US Navy's premier carrier-based fighter in 1942/43. It could dive faster and was of tougher construction than the Zero, its main opponent. The stubby Wildcat held the line until the arrival of the faster Hellcats in late 1943. A number have been restored, including an early service F4F-3 (above left and overleaf) and a main production version FM-2 (above right) which carries the "Felix-the-Cat" emblem of Fighting Squadron VF3. The modern trio is worth comparing to the wartime trio of F4F-3s.

The pre-war green-and-yellow eye-catching colours of Fighting Squadron VF4 (below) contrast with its wartime scheme (right). Wildcats also flew with the US Marine Corps and Royal Navy's Fleet Air Arm. At top right are three flying formation on an SB2C Helldiver.

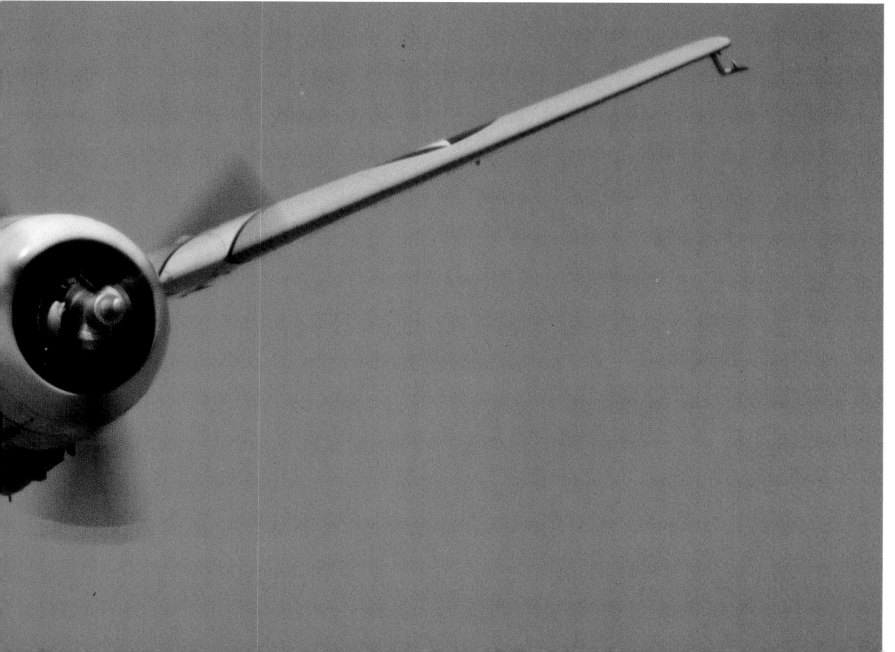

Known to many as "The Beast", the widely-used but least-loved Curtiss SB2C Helldiver was a replacement for the Dauntless. Well-armed, big and fast, it saw a lot of action with the large US fleet carriers. This quartet (top right) from USS *Ticonderoga* are returning from the last strike against Japan's home islands in August 1945. A SB2C-5 has been restored (top left, bottom right and overleaf) and is flown here by Nelson Ezell who pulls it around in a bank to demonstrate the size and smooth lines of this powerful machine.

The Chance Vought F4U Corsair was a gull-winged fighter of outstanding performance. The US Navy turned it down for carrier operations and it built its reputation flying for the Marine Corps from land bases in the Solomons (below, top and bottom). By 1944 the USN had realized their mistake and it increasingly supplemented the Hellcats. It went on to serve as a ground attack aircraft in Korea.

(Overleaf) The Corsair also became a successful radar-equipped night fighter and night-interdiction aircraft in Korea alongside the Tigercat.

The Fairey Firefly was a two seat, single-engine fighter for aircraft carrier operations. The rear seat was for an observer navigator deemed necessary by the British for long overseas patrols and reconnaissance purposes. This surviving version has 1944 European war markings, but another combat theatre was that patrolled by the British Pacific Fleet (top right).

(Previous page) The Grumman F7F Tigercat went into USMC service just too late to take part in WWII, but two squadrons saw heavy service in Korea. This immaculate single-seat version is owned by Plane Sailing.

A high-performing piston-engined fighter, the Hawker Sea Fury was just too late for WWII. It did, however, see service over Korea where it operated from British aircraft carriers (bottom left) and even managed a MiG-15 kill. Howard Pardue's aircraft has been restored to represent a land-based version, a role it performed for the Australian and Canadian navies.

The North American F-86 Sabre was the first US fighter to be developed with the benefit of captured German swept-wing technology. It arrived just in time to oppose the formidable MiG-15 over Korea. Many variants were built, ranging from the classic F-86F day fighter (top, left and right) to the F-86D all-weather and night-fighter seen below unleashing a salvo of "Mighty Mouse" rockets.

The Grumman F9F Panther was the first naval jet to enter combat, a number taking off from USS *Philippine* Sea on 6 August 1950 for a sortie over Korea (top right). Only one is airworthy (left, bottom right and overleaf); an F9F-2 painted to represent Fighting Squadron VF112, it carries rocket projectiles and wingtop auxiliary fuel tanks. The Panther was subsequently developed into the swept wing F9F-8 Cougar.

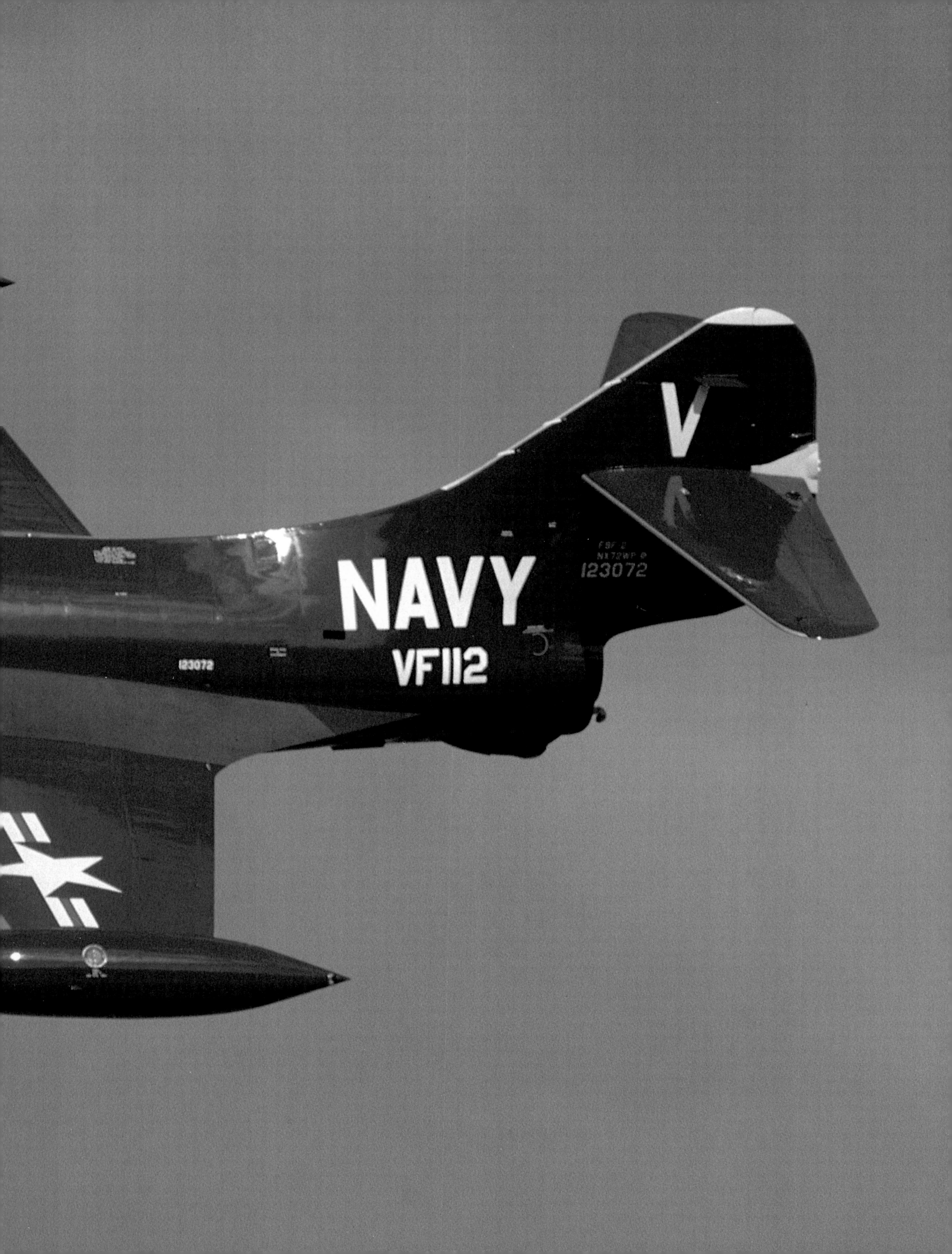
V
NAVY
VF112
123072
123072

Developed from the famous MiG-15, the MiG-17 was virtually the same fuselage and tail married to new wings of increased (45deg) sweepback. Entering service in 1952 it did not see combat until the Suez crisis of 1956. Later, it was used heavily by the North Vietnamese. A number have been sold in the US, mainly licence-built Chinese models such as this which performed at the Manchester Airshow, New Hampshire in 1990 (below, right and overleaf). At right is an all-weather, radar-equipped MiG17F in Russian service.

The Mikoyan-Gurevich
MiG-21 Fishbed (above, right
and overleaf) is one of the
most modern of the aircraft
appearing at airshows. Few
jet fighters have been built in
greater quantities than this
classic Russian delta which
has served long and reliably
with dozens of the world's air
forces and remains in front-
line service with many today.
The formation was staged by
visiting Soviet Air Force
MiG-21s at Upsala, Sweden in
the 1970s.

One of the longest serving front-line aircraft, the Douglas AD Skyraider was serving with 29 US Navy squadrons by 1955 and remained in use until 1968. It was very adaptable and a number of versions were built, culminating in the well-known A-1 of Vietnam fame (top right). Three restored Skyraiders were gathered at La Ferte Alois in June 1990 (right). The lead aircraft depicts Attack Squadron VA-176 operating from USS *Saratoga*, while the all-blue scheme is from USS *Hornet*.

The A4D Skyhawk was another durable aircraft from the Douglas stable. It replaced the Skyraider in US Navy and Marine service and was widely employed as an attack aircraft over Vietnam. This A-4 (left and overleaf) was once the mount of the US Navy's "Blue Angels" aerobatic team and is now owned by the Combat Jets Museum of Houston, Texas. The air-to-ground missile launch is from a two-seat trainer of the US Marines.